MW00770329

Dear Yvonne,

It's great to see parents

The Slacker's Guide to Success

who care so much
about their children
and want to be their
very best.
Enjoy your hero's journey
and lead

Ken Rabow

by your great example.

Ken Rebow

The Slacker's Guide to Success

Ken Rabow

KNR PUBLISHING

With grateful assistance from speaks&spells publishing

ISBN: 978-0-9918785-0-5

1.Self-help/Personal Coaching 2.Teen and Young
Adult 3.Daily Routines and Life Structuring

Copyright © Ken Rabow 2013. KNR Publishing.

All rights reserved. No part of this publication may be reproduced or
transmitted in any form or by any means, electronic or mechanical,
including photocopying, recording, or any information storage and
retrieval system, without permission in writing from the publisher.

Notes

This book belongs to:

_____

I love writing notes in blank pages of books I am reading, so I have added a space for you to jot down any notes you'd like to make. Feel free to write down any of your own ideas as well! ~ KNR

Date	Page	Idea

Ken Rabow

Date	Page	Idea

Please note the following things:

All quotations that appear in this book are considered in the public domain. No breaking of copyright is intended.

As to the source material used here... while these are examples taken from my experiences with my clients, no one client's story is portrayed. Confidentiality is the cornerstone of my practice and I would never betray the trust put in me. The examples are an amalgam of a number of real-life experiences and difficulties with which I am grateful to have been an agent of change.

Table of Contents

Stage Two: Professional Development

Stage Three

Acknowledgments

I want to thank every student, every client, and every parent I have worked with for all they have taught me; for letting their faith in me allow them to try things that were vastly different from what they were used to. I want to thank them for taking a chance on themselves and learning to see within the greatness I saw in them.

I want to thank my editor, Susan Hargrove, who has been an inspiration, helping me to find the bestest way to articulate what I have learned from my clients and how to share this with the world at large. Her love of the English language and her counsel keeping me "on track" is one of the reasons that you are reading this book.

I want to thank my sister, Rhonda, for all her support and care throughout the years and my brother, Bill, for inspiring me to be my best. I want to thank my best friend and best man, Steve G., for always having my back and for sharing a love of the comedy classics and corny humour.

I have been blessed with so many great and constant friends over the years who have been with me through many of my incarnations in this life. You know who you are and I thank you from the bottom of my heart.

I want to thank my Mom, Ethel Rabow, for her wisdom, her sense of humour, and her dignity until the very end. You are sorely missed.

Most importantly, I want to thank my beautiful, soulful, wise, and plain-spoken wife, Helena. She has always believed in me, always let me know when enough is enough, and who still dances with me though our hallways in joy. None of my accomplishments would ring with love if you weren't in my life. Helena, you are my friend, my love, and my compass.

Finally, to the Infinite Spirit, the Creator: I have such thankfulness in my heart for the gifts you bring to me and all of the people with whom I share my thoughts and observations. I feel you walking every step with me and I hear you in my heart. I thank you for staying with me when I lose my way into my own selfishness and I thank you for being in my heart when I witness growth in the people around me.

Dude, why are you still reading this stuff… move on to page 1, already! Go for it!

Introduction

Where you are and where you are going

So, you know you're brilliant, your parents know you're brilliant, and your dog thinks you're amazing; why are so many things in your life not working out?

Hi. My name is Ken Rabow and I work with teens and young adults struggling to find their place in the world. The ones I take on as clients are those who really want to make changes in their lives. Many of the clients I work with come to me when they have…

a. Been stuck in part-time jobs without a future.
b. Become addicted to video games, or pot, or magic cards, or something else.
c. Failed school.
d. Major sleep or anger issues.
e. All of the above.

Don't you just love multiple choice?!?

One of my clients once said to me: "I really like staying at home, playing video games all day in my bathrobe… but I'm beginning to think that it's not a great long-term plan."

Let us call that client Skeeter. At the time of the writing of this book,

Skeeter is back in school working on a science degree. In his first semester, he caught the attention of an amazing professor doing ground-breaking research who has now hired Skeeter to work in the lab.

So how did Skeeter go from being a stay-in-his room slacker to an up-and-coming science guy? And what about you? What if you are into something other than video games but just as slack? What if you don't want to go to school but have dreams of starting your own business or creating a killer app?

So, why should you care? Because ☺.

Okay, that's a parent-y answer. The real answer is that what worked for Skeeter can work for you—in any field, in any format, in any situation.

Your success will come from:

- Finding your power.
- Learning to believe in yourself.
- Determining how to build habits that guarantee success.
- Discovering the secret to success through messing up.

Yes, I'm here to tell you that you can't really be great at anything until you can get past… perfectionism.

That's what this system is all about. And it works! Each time. Every time. I've seen so many young people change their lives around. There are a lot of people out there who deserve to learn how to be their very best and do great things with their lives. I've written this book so that more of you could benefit from the "out-of-the-box" process I've refined in my private practice over the years. This process that will enable you to succeed on your own terms. If you follow this method, you'll find yourself growing in character and soon enough you will discover yourself achieving successes you didn't dare dream of. You will find that it's great to get out of bed every morning, feeling good about doing things that earn people's respect. More importantly, you will feel good about yourself for your personal achievements.

You will learn how to get people to give you what you want by giving them what they need. Most people really want to be heard. I mean really heard. People aren't just killing time when they talk (hard to believe, I know); they actually have something to say. They want you to listen to them; but more than that, they want to know that you understood them and that you empathize with what they are saying. If you can do that, then the world is your oyster (if you like oysters).

And check this out! Most teachers actually like it when a student comes to them and asks how they can do better than they did on the last test or project. Those awe-struck teachers will tell you what you need to do to win grades. It ain't magic; it's school logic. And in the end, you will know exactly what to do and the precise amount of effort you need to put in to get better grades.

And by listening to your parents and having your first actual conversation that doesn't feel like you are in court or bizzaro-land (most likely, they feel the same way), double down with your improved grades and they will be much more open to any ideas you may want to run by them. ("Hey Mom! What d'ya think about getting me that amazing new portable hovercraft for getting to school?" "Whatever you say, Skeeter!")

How this system works

How does this system work and how does it not work? Well, it doesn't work by reading it, or meditating on it, or telling your friends how good it is (but please do); it doesn't work by promising to start after the next killer video game hits the streets and you've played up to level gazillion. It works by doing it. Just start! Read the first step and then do the work!

Here's another way it doesn't work. It doesn't work alone. You will need someone's help. I strongly recommend someone who is not your parent, your guardian, or your Auntie Bert who lives in the basement. That's right. A neighbour, a distant relative, or a mentor volunteer from a local institution: a religious institution, a community centre, or a place where the guys wear hats with those dangly things on them. Most importantly, find someone you can talk to, someone who will keep your secrets, someone who will respect you, and let you grow at your own pace.

The best way to get a mentor: have one of your parents mentor an acquaintance outside of your circle of friends and have one of their parents mentor you. I will explain this process further in Step Two.

How this book works

This book is divided into three stages. Each Stage represents one full phase of development in this system. The first is personal development. The second Stage, professional development, has you taking what you've learned out into the world with your newly honed strengths. The third Stage, inner development, focuses on your taking all you've learned and all you've become and using it to grow as a person and give back to the world.

They say when you point a finger at someone and accuse them of something, three fingers point back at you. I've found the same is true about helping people. Think of Michelangelo's famous "Creation of Adam." When you put out even one finger to help someone else, you get three fingers of help back from the universe. It just works. That's the idea behind Stage Three.

Within the book are 13 Steps that take you through the three Stages. Each Step is a concentrated focus point to give you direction, to keep you on your journey towards success. Here is a brief outline of what each Step involves.

If you have questions or want more information on this or the following books on the subject, you can reach me by going to www.reallifecoaching. ca or e-mail any questions you may have to sgts@reallifecoaching.ca

Introducing Stages and Steps

Stage One—Personal Development

Step One: Investigation. A life that is investigated becomes a life worth living. We begin by looking at our strengths and the challenges we face in harnessing those strengths. We look at our past patterns of self-sabotage and find the coping strategies we use to "deal" with the world. We then learn how to choose role models, events, or ideas as inspiration to guide us into being our better selves day by day, moment by moment.

Step Two: Opportunity. Opportunities are all around us. We need to know how to recognize them and how to say "yes" to the ones that will benefit us. We will learn how to choose a mentor and how to enlist that mentor into helping us set goals, define the challenges to reaching those goals, and determine how we measure our first level of success.

Step Three: Mindsets. Our mindset is the lens through which we shape how we live our lives. When people see the positive possibilities in a given situation, they are engaging in an abundance mindset. When people see only what is lacking in certain parts of their lives, this is the poverty mindset at play. We will look at the places in our lives where we have an "abundance mindset" and the places where we have a "poverty mindset" and we will focus on bringing abundance to all aspects of our lives while learning how to avoid the negative thoughts that can stop changes.

Step Four: Generativity. Here we learn how to create a daily routine— our personal meaningful practice. As we implement our daily routine, we experience the blocks that prevent our successes and learn to find ways around those blocks.

Step Five: Out into the world (and back again). We now put our new skills into practice in the outside world in a safe way for a short, defined period of time.

Step Six: How to arrest your time stealers. We learn how to set limits gracefully on the time-stealers in our lives.

Step Seven: Direction (following your bliss). This is where we lay the groundwork for a successful, enjoyable life doing what we were meant to do in this lifetime.

Stage Two—Professional Development

Step Eight: Three toes in the water. At this point, we engage in a more extended practice of the things we learned in Stage One. It could be going to university or college, it could be entering the work force, the art world, or it could be taking steps towards creating an entrepreneurial business. We apply what we have learned into new and broader situations.

Step Nine: Feeling safe "out there." Using the practice of being mindful in our daily lives, we look at our recent successes and see how they can work in new situations while we learn to feel safe "out there."

Step Ten: From Crud to Cred: creating new generative structures. Building on our work, we focus on schedules, on coping, and on making new friends who will re-enforce our successes.

Step Eleven: Making your addictions work for you. We find creative ways to use our impulses as rewards for doing the work we need to get done and becoming Masters of our own domain.

Stage Three—Inner Development

Step Twelve: Living a full life. We begin a sustainable daily practice of being mindful in learning, work, relationships, and play. Creating a full and successful life secure with the knowledge that any future stumbling blocks will become mere stepping stones to even greater accomplishments.

Step Thirteen: Helping others helps you. Once we've reached this point, our life is richer, we are happier, and we truly want to help others grow in their own way. This step will teach us how to do that.

Stage One
Personal Development

Here is the question that I am seldom asked, yet it rests in the hearts and minds of every client who crosses my doorstep waiting to begin their journey through this first Stage: "Why do I have to suffer so! What is the point of all these challenges in my life, and why isn't my life as easy and fulfilling as everybody else's life?" Maybe it's a good thing that they don't ask because they might take a slug at me if they heard my answer. Here it is: Every challenge and every failure that comes into your life is an opportunity to find your greatness. So many of the people of substance we admire in life have risen above tremendous tribulations. They had one important advantage that many do not: a daily routine of personal contemplation, physical exercise, and creative outlets. These are the building blocks of a deep inner-faith in oneself. In Stage One, you will learn to take on these attributes so you may find the path towards your true inner potential.

Step One

Investigation of Strengths and Challenges

You can change your life for the better right now!

Changing your life starts with looking at the strengths and challenges you face each day in your life. By examining your challenges, you can start to see the patterns that you repeat and the self-limiting thoughts running in your subconscious: "I'll never be able to do that… Why bother doing ***, etc." Our strengths can inspire us to rise above these repeating patterns and thoughts; they lead us towards living a richer life. You can learn to change that nagging voice in your head to an inspirational coach. This chapter will help you begin making that transformation.

- Your strengths can help you do well in your daily life.
- Your challenges are the gateway to your genius.
- So many people have talents that they either don't believe in or too easily dismiss.

In order to change your life around, in order to not only achieve success but also earn praise, respect, and eventually a rewarding income, you need to believe in yourself. Most of the work of Stage One in this book is about learning to have faith in yourself and gain pride in your "quiet accomplishments."

Quiet accomplishments are those things that you work on without the world noticing. They aren't done to show off or receive praise but are done to feel good about yourself. They are just as challenging as the things others see, but when you do them well, there's a deep inner pride that will be nourished and will keep growing.

Let me tell you about Wendy.

When Wendy came to me and I asked her what she was good at, she looked deep into my eyes with tears beginning to well up and replied: "Nothing." I was taken aback. "Isn't there something you like doing that you're good at?" I asked her.

"Well," she said, "I paint with watercolours and I can make a picture of whatever I see and people tell me it looks just like the real thing, but better."

"Don't you think that this is something you can say that you are good at?" I inquired.

Wendy then told me her deep belief: "I just know that anyone can do it, so it's not really special."

This reminded me of my one foray into the world of drawing. My kindergarten teacher sent me home one day with my class colouring book. She wrote in big red letters across it: "Kenny will never learn to colour inside the lines! It's impossible!" My mom read the note to me, folded the note three times and then exclaimed: "Well you know, Ken, you are the very best at drawing outside the lines that I have ever seen!"

I told Wendy that I could never draw like her and would give my eyeteeth to be able to draw the way she did.

She looked at me with genuine surprise, "You can't?"

"Most people can't," I said.

She looked confused and a little uncertain of what that meant. Then I asked her: "If most people can't do it and you do it really well, what does that tell you?"

"I guess it is something that I'm good at," sighed Wendy. And with that we began the reshaping of her deep beliefs.

Before you can reach the point of creating a daily practice to change your limiting deep beliefs, you will have to create goals and uncover the challenges to those goals.

I want you to imagine for the moment that you are in my studio on my very relaxing, comfy, and safe couch. I'm on the other side of the room in my chair. You are my client and I would like you to try some exercises.

Exercise One: Goals

- Goals: Take a moment and write down three things that you want to work on.
- Obstacles: What would you say are some of the challenges you see to making these goals become your reality? Write down at least one challenge for each goal and then put a number from one to ten to indicate your level of desire to resolve this obstacle and reach that particular goal.

The scale is this:

- Ten would indicate the most important goal of your life.
- Seven, a very important goal.
- Five being a take-it-or-leave-it goal.
- Anything below that, diminishing in interest all the way down to one.
- Finally, use the in-between numbers as shadings in between these levels.
- Success: Write down one line describing what you think would be a good indication of positive progress towards each goal.

You can download a version of these questions here:
http://www.reallifecoaching.ca/rlc/Initial_Questionnaire.html

Here are real-world goals, obstacles, and success markers from Skeeter.

Please state three things you wish to work on:

1. Procrastination
2. Social Skills (Not to feel "awkward" when I talk to people)
3. Finding my own path to success

What would you say are some of the challenges you have to making these things be as you want them to be?

(After the explanation, please put a number from 1–10 indicating your level of desire to resolve the situation.)

1. I always find excuses not to get started. It seems much harder once you have been procrastinating. This is an 8.
2. I'm very shy when it comes to doing something in public. I worry about them "thinking" something bad about me. This is a 10.
3. I dread trying "something" new. I'm afraid I might flunk out again. This is a 7.

What would be a good indicator that you have made progress in each of these things?

1. When I start seeing myself actively "pursuing" something that needs to be done without anyone telling me to.
2. When I'm saturated by a large group of people and I'm able to really talk.
3. When I get the feeling that my life is getting on the right track.

Something very powerful happens when you write down your challenges and strengths. They take on a power and meaning that thinking or talking about them cannot reach. Once written, they become objects you can build up, modify, or let go of at will. You become the one in control of them; you become the Master of your own fate.

Take a moment to look over your goals. More often than not, I find my clients put those goals in the exact order of importance. But importance isn't necessarily the best place to start. Look at your three goals and decide which goal inspires you the most. This is the one you should start with. Once you get the first goal moving towards your indicator for success, you will know which one should follow. Remember, your goals can change; they grow and evolve. The important thing is to set your mind on a target and go for it.

Now inspect your obstacles. Do they accurately represent your stumbling blocks? Do they need to be modified or are they good as they are? Chances are that you nailed them perfectly (and for those of you who didn't bother to actually write them down... do so now! No, really... I'm watching... that's better!)

Check out your choice of indicators for success. By choosing an indicator for success, you are allowing your whole mind to consider success. Once your minds, both the conscious and subconscious, are in sync and are considering the possibility of success, you will make constant micro-decisions that you may not even notice making. These micro-decisions, will guide you towards your successes.

Moving now to your strengths, we shall discover the tools you need to rise above your challenges.

Exercise Two: Strengths

- *Talent:* Write down something that you are good at. It may be what you know you do well or it may be something that comes easily to you but you dismiss it because, like Wendy, you think "anyone can do that." Both of those are strengths. List as many as you can think of. As long as you have at least one, you are on your way.

- *Inspiration:* Think of a person you admire who is either still living or someone from the past whom you believe to be inspiring. When you find yourself in a frustrating situation, ask yourself: "What would they do?" It's okay to change that person from time to time depending on which skill (resolving conflict, inspiring others, working as a team, etc.) or quality (passion, caring, humility, etc.) you wish to draw down into yourself.

- ***Power Place:*** Imagine a situation or a place that makes you feel powerful. It could be something you've seen or heard about. It could be something you hope will one day happen. Use your strongest senses to try to make it feel real. Imagine what it would feel like to be experiencing it right now. I had one client who would picture himself in a spotlight waiting for his song to begin in front of a huge crowd. He pictured the stadium. He could smell the excitement and hear the crowd. He could feel them waiting for him to begin and he was ready. That was his power place.

Remember… nothing is cast in stone. As you move forward in this method, you may end up modifying what you have written down in these first exercises. This re-evaluation is expected.

A great film director was once asked what was the most important quality for a leader. He said: "the ability to make an immediate decision." It didn't matter whether it was the right or wrong choice because he knew whatever it was, it could be corrected. The crew sensed his decisiveness, and with that they could relax and do their jobs, knowing there was direction.

The same is true of our subconscious. It is that crew waiting to be led and our will becomes the director. So choose your goals and choose your strengths knowing that making the choice itself propels you forward towards success. If you find these choices don't suit you after you have given them your best effort, then go back and modify or change them.

Now, let's go on to what you do with what you've written down. The following are some exercises you can start with tomorrow.

Daily Practice:

1. Choose a goal
   a. Choose one goal that you wish to work on first from your three goals. You may want to do them in order but you may choose to start with any one of the three.
   b. Reflect on the obstacle that is in your way. What kind of obstacle is it? It is a belief stopping you? Is it a fear? Rate it on a scale from one to ten of erasability.

This is the scale:

- Ten would indicate something that could be completely erased.

- Seven an obstacle that would have very little hold on you.
- Five being a level where half the time you would be free of it.
- Anything below that are obstacles that would be harder and harder to erase.
- Use the in-between numbers as shadings in between these levels.

   c. "Soften" the obstacle. Pick three points of attack you can use to minimize your obstacle. Call these points your aspects. Work on one aspect each and every day until you begin to see that aspect of the obstacle melting away. Move on to the next aspect until they are all gone. When you have made it through the three aspects of your first obstacle, carry onto the next challenge. It sometimes helps to have an outside person work on this with you. We shall talk about that in the next step.

2. Imagine your power place. Each night just before falling asleep, close your eyes and imagine experiencing your power place. If you are doing something there, *live it* as if it was happening to you right now. Take in every feeling of it. Be open to things that will happen during the following day of doing this practice, things that bring you closer to making your power place a reality.

3. Reflect on your inspiration: When you wake up, take a moment to reflect on one quality of your inspirational person. Decide to implement that quality at least once today.

4. Keep a journal. Write down between one sentence to one page about what is going on in your life each day. "Why should I?" A very good question! Many of these changes are subtle. By journaling daily, you track the subtleties. All of my clients are amazed when they look back over a few months of entries and see the real improvements that have come about in their thoughts and actions.

There you have it. Work on these exercises until you feel you have a good command of them, then take a look at the next Step.

"The longest journey begins with a single step."

~ Lao-tzu ~

Carrying on with Skeeter, here is his example for softening obstacles on one of his goals.

Choose a goal to work on:

Social Skills (Not to feel "awkward" when I talk to people)

Write down three obstacles in your way of the goal.

Write down if it is a belief (something you have experienced before; a fear (something that never has happened but you are afraid may happen); other (explain what that is).

Use the scale from 1–10 (10 being easy to "melt," 1 being close to impossible) and put a number next to it.

1. I'm very shy when it comes to doing something in public. This is a belief and I give it a 5.
2. I worry about them thinking something bad about me. This is a fear and I give it a 7.
3. I tend not to know when to stop talking and I can see people's eye glaze over, but I can't stop myself. This is a belief and I give it an 8.5.

Soften the obstacles. Pick three points of attack to soften.

(Here is the example for obstacle 1. See if you can figure out three "softening points" for Skeeter's 2nd and 3rd obstacles.

1. My belief that I'm very shy when it comes to doing something in public.
   a. (Shy) Try and see how many people are confident in a public situation and how many people are nervous. Make it your goal to help a nervous person feel comfortable.
   b. See if there is something neat about them: how they look, how they hold themselves, their laugh, their voice and give them an honest compliment.
   c. See what it feels like to walk into a room acting as if you were confident and imagine being open to talking to people.
   d. Volunteer to help someone in the group who is seeking help.

2. My fear about them "thinking" something bad about me.

    a. _____

       _____

    b. _____

       _____

    c. _____

       _____

3. My belief that I talk too much.

    a. _____

       _____

    b. _____

       _____

    c. _____

       _____

Step Two

Opportunity: Choosing A Mentor and Establishing Goals

You now have:

- Your Goals.
- Your Challenges.
- Your Indicators for Success.
- Your Power Place.
- Your Inspirational Character or Event.

You have done some work on your own and that is great. Now it's time to take it up to the next level. For this, you need guidance, guidance in the form of an outside party who is not caught up in the day-to-day consequences of your life. You want someone who will be able to be an unbiased coaching presence on your journey to self-empowerment.

Apprenticeships and Mentors

For most of recorded history, between the ages of ten and 15 you left your family to either become an apprentice to a tradesman, join the army, work on someone's farm, or if you were from "privileged class," you were given over to an educator. In all these situations, you went from learning life lessons from the family to the learning how to succeed in the world by working along side of a mentor. This was the way it was for thousands of years until the mid-1700s when philosopher Jean-Jacques Rousseau proposed a treatise on the education of children. This proposition offered the opportunity of formal education to young people. Later on, child labour laws came into effect, protecting more young people and saving many from lives as labourers or indentured servants.

With the decline of apprenticeships, we have lost appreciation for the powerful and positive influence that an outside one-on-one mentor can have on the success of a young person. We foisted all of these duties onto the parents and extended family. Times changed again and many people only saw extended family on weekends and holidays. As we became satellite nuclear families, we off-loaded the responsibilities of mentoring onto teachers and officials. To this day, we have come to expect parents, teachers, sports coaches and, in some cases, judges to be all things to all children. But to succeed, a young person needs a number of people with a wide range of varied experiences and mindsets from whom they may learn. From these models, a person can choose individual life lessons he or she will put into action to create his or her own path. Young people who don't participate in any of the standard activities where coaches can be found: sports, dance, theatre, martial arts, etc., have fewer opportunities for learning from a wider-range of mentors/coaches. For the young people who do not fit into the standard mould, seeking out a personal mentor becomes a worthwhile endeavour.

Many clients with whom I have worked chose me to be their mentor and together we have succeeded beyond their expectations and gone past their fears. People who take their fate into their own hands, who find the right guiding examples and put together a good starting strategy, are on a powerful path towards success.

There are many skills you will need. Some you have, some will need nurturing, and some will need to be acquired. It is important to remember that the one thing that can change between today and tomorrow are the people you meet and the books you read. These opportunities for inspiration can form lasting impressions on us that are life-changing and life affirming.

The following is a guide to finding the proper mentor for you.

To choose the proper mentor, you must first take a close look at yourself. Analyze who you are and how you do things best. Knowing who you are, what works and what doesn't is the first step in choosing someone to mentor you. You are in charge of your life. You may just not know it yet.

Self Assessment:

1. **Learning Style:** Write down the ways that you best learn. Is it by seeing something done (visual), by hearing it explained (auditory), or by the physicality of doing it (kinaesthetic)? Although most people are visually dominant in their learning style, not everyone is. Your dominant style maybe auditory (I hear you) or kinaesthetic (I feel what you mean). Whatever your dominant style is, it is the one you most often use to learn. Your learning styles will range in order of importance from most to least. Number your learning styles in order of importance: Visual ____, Auditory ____, Kinaesthetic____.

2. **Intuitive, Logical, or Both:** Go to a mirror and look at the distance between your lower eyelids and upper eyelids. One of your eyes will be open more than the other. If your left eyelids are more open, you are an intuitive learner; if it is the right set of eyelids, you are a logic-based learner. There is a third option. Check out which eye is open more in the mirror periodically for a whole day. If you see yourself switching dominant eyes, you are someone who alternates using both hemispheres of your brain, learning using both logic and intuition. Logical learners want the instruction book, intuitive learners want to know how it works and they'll make up their own instructions. People who can alternate between hemispheres end up with one of two scenarios: either they are great at school and working with their logic and intuition—matching the hemisphere required at the time with the task at hand—or they have big problems in school—not knowing which hemisphere they should use for which task. The latter learners tend not to know how to retrieve the information easily. Over a period of a day, observe which eye is dominant (or if you switch) and then fill in the following: Logic-based (Right eye) ____, Intuitive-based (Left eye) ____, Both Hemispheres ____.

3. **Success in Learning:** Look back to a time when you learned something that you did well. It could be the simplest of things in your mind but by using the methods explained above, examine how you learned. Remember: use what works. You may choose other ways to learn but always start with ones that have served you well in the past.

One of the best things you can do before you chose someone to coach/mentor you is know yourself. Be honest about your strengths and weaknesses and be prepared to share these confidentially with your mentor. This is the beginning of self knowledge.

Problem Solving. What do you do when things mess up and your efforts fail to give you the outcome you hoped for? Circle the letter which represents your "go to" system.

Do you:

a. Just keeping doing the same thing until it works.

b. Try something completely different and forget about whatever it was that didn't work.

c. Blame someone or something.

d. Blame yourself.

e. Analyze what went wrong and why (even guessing). Learn from it and then try something based on what you learned.

Most people usually start with "c" or "d." That is a natural place to start. Often they then move on to "b" and so many are type "a's" that it's scary. The correct answer here is "e." Every time there is a setback, a mistake, or a failure, you may feel bad or temporarily defeated but that is a feeling and you can choose to let go of that feeling once you are ready to. If you "reboot" yourself, you will see that you are being given a marvellous opportunity to learn and grow. You may learn a different way to approach whatever it is that you are trying to do or you may find a whole new path that you would never had considered with out the dreaded mis-take.

People who make films know that film-making is not created as a solid running narrative of the final story that will be shown but as a series of segments or "takes." Very often each take can be done many times to get it just right. What would happen if the first time they had a mis-take, they packed up their equipment and went home? We would never see a film again! What is also interesting is that some of the best parts of films or a new idea on how to produce a part of the film come from these mis-takes.

I suggest that we become the director/producer of the film that is our life. Let's use our mis-takes to become our best selves. This is the ultimate in problem solving. It is in the mistakes that we can often find the exceptional. Whatever we do, we are either succeeding or learning. By understanding how you learn, how you solve problems, and how to draw power from mis-takes, you are ready to find someone to work with and share your understanding of how you "work" best.

Choosing a Mentor

In choosing a mentor, you are looking for someone who can listen to you and guide you without getting in the way. Someone who will let you walk your own path and turn you around before you hit a dead end. The path must be walked by you alone. The mentor is there as an outside, non-judgmental voice. Here are some qualities to keep in mind on your search for a mentor:

- **1st Quality: Do They Know you?** They must understand you; they must understand how you learn and how you problem solve. With so many learning styles, a mentor who does not take the time to understand how you learn has a 1/16 chance of being the right teacher for you (that's 6.25%). What worked for someone else doesn't mean it will work for you.

  If they talk about themselves and how good they are... Run! If they seem to really "get" you... Stay!

- **2nd Quality: A Person of Valour.** The role of a mentor is to guide you towards learning to own your natural talents. Therefore, your mentor should be someone who you respect. Character is the thing we are searching for; character cannot be copied but it can inspire us to be our best when being best isn't easy. Make sure this mentor is a person of valour.

- **3rd Quality: A Good Listener.** Active listening is an art. The ability to listen, to give meaningful feedback, to empathize, and to validate is something of a lost art. Make sure your mentor has this quality. It's easy to spot. Tell them something you haven't shared before and see if they "get it."

- **4th Quality: Action.** All of the above qualities are powerful but without a plan of action, they are merely ideas. Ideas without action will never get you onto the path towards your personal success. Your mentor must be the kind of person willing to help you implement goals based on the three first qualities stated above. Goals without understanding go nowhere; understanding without goals never gets out of the gate. Action is the vehicle for combining your goals with your understanding, and infusing them with life from the real world.

Now that you have done a full self-assessment and selected a mentor based on the above stated qualities, it's time to share your plan with your mentor.

Sharing Your Plan:

a. Goals

Share the goals you have chosen in Step One. Give your mentor your thoughts as to what each goal represents in your life. Be open to feedback.

b. Challenges

Clarify the challenges within you that may interfere with your reaching your goals. Expand on each of the challenges and the experiences that you have had in working on them on your own. The process should always be one of give and take. Your mentor is there to present options to you that you may not have considered.

c. Success Markers

Make crystal clear what the indicator is that tells you you are succeeding in each of these goals. Always keep in mind that your mentor is someone who is guiding you but that inevitably, you are the one who must be the captain of this voyage towards your own destiny.

d. Communication and Steering the Boat

This is your journey. You should be the one to make the ultimate decisions with your mentor offering counsel. Make sure you express what your desires and fears are and if your mentor is going somewhere that you do not wish to go, state your concerns and steer the boat back toward your course. Your mentor may be right in the long run but you learn best by following your inner wisdom and understanding. Make sure you are willing to make changes should your course need correcting.

This is the work to do with your mentor. See it as a daring adventure to find yourself far from the shores of what is safe and easy.

I strongly recommend that you keep a Success Journal of all your learning information, your daily practices, and your thoughts. You can download the Success Journal I use with my clients by going to this URL:

http://www.reallifecoaching.ca/RealLifeCoaching/Success_Journal.html

"Security is mostly a superstition. It does not exist in nature nor do the children of man as a whole experience it. Avoiding danger is no safer in the long run than outright exposure. Life is either a daring adventure, or nothing."

~ Helen Keller ~

Step Three

Mindsets

Blaine had all the talent required to be an outstanding runner. He had a great stance; he ran like the wind and could go for miles. But he always faltered at the finish line, coming in 3rd or 4th even though he had the lead at the ¾ mark in each and every race. Time after time as he was reaching the end and victory was in his grasp, Blaine would look back and slow down. Once more the others who had been behind him would pass him by.

It turns out Blaine had always been fast for his age but an incident, unbeknownst to his parents and so long ago in time that Blaine could barely remembered it, had limited his ability to succeed. At six years old, Blaine had challenged one of the "big kids" on the street to a race. As the race began Blaine shot ahead as usual and this made the big kid angry. As they got towards the end of the block, the big kid tripped Blaine and reached the goal first, laughing and taunting Blaine.

How could a memory buried so deep and mostly forgotten have such a powerful effect throughout someone's life? These instances that limit our abilities to succeed in one way or the other are called "false epiphanies." False epiphanies are moments from a painful time in our youth, where we decided to become self-limiting in order to protect ourselves.

For Blaine, it was: "if I am winning, someone will be right behind me to trip me up" or

"If I succeed, x won't like me" or

"If kids are only my friends because I succeed, I don't need friends" or

"It's always my x who succeeds; no one cares how I do" or

"Why bother, I can't succeed anyway" or

"If I try and fail again, it will hurt too much."

Fill in your own self-limiting belief here:

_____

At some point in our childhood, we have experienced negative incidents that caused us to become self-limiting. These self-limitations become recordings playing in our heads so often that we don't even notice what they are saying anymore and yet they effect every decision we make. Once we can discover these subconscious beliefs, **we can change these childhood tapes to self-empowerment and we then become free to make new healthy choices.**

Here is an example of changing the tapes:

- Pick something that you say to yourself over and over again that is self-limiting, e.g.: "I can't x," "I'll never be able to do y," "Everyone seems to be able to z except me," etc.

- Now imagine that you are the perfect coach and this person (you) is your client. What if that coach had heard the self-limiting belief being said aloud? How would they assess it? If that thought was removed, what possibilities for success would your client have?

- Picture how they could succeed: What daily routines would it take? What belief in themselves would it take? What would they have to hear from you if, when they tried, it didn't work at first?

Choose one sentence to say for each of these.

    a. Write them down.

    b. Go to a mirror and look into your eyes. Have the coach part of yourself tell the child part of yourself these positive words for a few minutes every day. Picture what it would feel like to succeed this way. Feel how you would feel and make that feeling something deep inside you that you can draw upon at any time. Hear the sounds that would accompany that success.

c. Imagine all the things that would accompany that success. The way you live. The car you drive. The people in your life. The clothes you wear. How you eat. How you spend your free time. Go into the greatest detail and imagine it as if it were happening right now.

Now for an example. Let's volunteer Blaine ☺.

FE: (False epiphany): "If I am winning, someone will be right behind me to trip me up"

CY: (Coach You) So, you are afraid that if you are winning, something unseen will come along and sabotage you?

FE: Yup. Big time.

CY: Do you know that this will, in fact, happen?

FE: Not really but it sure seems like it always happens.

CY: Can you give me an example of a time when this last happened?

FE: Well, I was, like, starting to teach people guitar and I had five students and things were going well and I was making money and all of a sudden, they all just left. I'm so sure that someone said something mean about me to them or wished me ill will.

CY: Could it be that there was another reason that they all stopped.

FE: (Mumbles) I dunno.

CY: When did they all stop?

FE: At the end of school. At the summer break.

CY: Did you try calling them back after school started?

FE: What's the point? I'm obviously not good at teaching.

CY: Did anyone say that you weren't good at teaching guitar?

FE: (Thinking back) No.

CY: Did they ever do things you were proud of?

FE: Well, I did get them playing a lot better than when they came to me.

CY: So, you don't know that anyone said any bad things about you or sabotaged you?

FE: No.

CY: And you never called these students back or tried again because you thought they were against you?

FE: Nu-uh.

CY: Would you agree that what you thought was not facts but guesses?

FE: I guess so [ignore the irony].

CY: You don't know the real facts because you never tried to find out if your guesses were real or fears from the past, true?

FE: True.

CY: If those students got better, the only real fact we know is that you are a good guitar teacher, right?

FE: I guess.

CY: Let's pretend for the moment that you really are as good a guitar teacher as you seem to be.

Since the idea that someone talked to these people is only a guess, let's leave it off the table for the moment and focus on what we know and imagine what we could do with what we do know.

CY: (Picture how you could succeed.) You are a good guitar teacher, with six great students, and all of them really enjoy learning guitar.

Imagine letting people know that you teach guitar, calling back old students from the past and inviting them to take guitar lessons from you.

(Belief in themselves.) Everyday take a few moments to say to yourself in the mirror: "I am a very good guitar teacher and I will find and keep the right student who will benefit from us working together."

CY: Let's write these down.

- I am a good teacher. I welcome good students.
- It takes a lot of talking to people to find the right students.
- I won't give up no matter what because I believe in myself.

(When you meet with failure.) Remember that you have to talk to ten people who want to take lessons to get one to really do it. Even if it takes 100 people to get that next student, you won't give up because the more you try and the more you believe that you will succeed, the more good clients you will get, the more they will stay with you because they know you have something to offer them.

You have now moved from poverty consciousness (lack) to abundance consciousness (you can do anything if you keep trying). Keep doing this every day and you will find that you automatically start making micro-decisions that bring you closer and closer to your successes.

It isn't quick. It isn't easy, but it works.

"Develop success from failures. Discouragement and failure are two of the surest stepping stones to success."

~ Dale Carnegie ~

Step Four

Generativity

A great sage once said:

> When one reaches the end of one's life and goes to the great equalizer in the sky, one will not be asked 'why did you not have the determination of Gandhi?' or 'why did you not match the greatness of Abraham Lincoln?'; one will be asked **'why were you not the best "you" that you could be?'**

So many young people live their lives through their computers; texting, e-mailing, bbm-ing so much that face time, the actual time they are face to face with people becomes less and less part of their social lives. And when it comes to family communication, how many kids are being texted by their parents while they are both in the very same house?

We end up with the "bathrobe syndrome." If most of us are connecting through our digital words, why bother getting dressed… or shaving… or brushing our teeth? Might as well stay unbathed in our Snuggies. To continue that thought, if our physical appearance is no longer meaningful and all that is important are our words, **how much do our words mean when we can delete them or delete an unappreciated reply so that it is as if it never happened?**

Then, why bother? (Have you heard that question before?)

We need to own what we do. The truth is that it is the things we do just for ourselves, things that we do on a daily basis, things we do when we are inspired but also when we are sick of doing them, that are the things which build character and create something I call **Generativity.** I am defining **generativity as things one does to improve the quality of life in any way, moment by moment.**

The first Step in Generativity is daily organization.

1. An organized workspace: Make sure that everything you can see when you are looking at your work-space is clutter-free.

2. Clean lookin' and clean smellin': There is a knock on your door. It's Doctor Kildare and it's time for your annual physical. (This hypothetical doctor also makes house calls.) No prob. You are ready and good to go.

3. Honourable in public and in private: Unbeknownst to you, little sister put a secret webcam in your room. Unbeknownst to her, nothing worthy of YouTube will happen anymore.

But wait! There's more! I call it "the daily routine." (Tell us more, Ken!)

It is the daily routine that will help you "own" your life. It is a model that, once you have it down, will be useful in helping empower you in all parts of your life. Basically, it is the one thing that can transform your life for the better and have you be the one earning each small victory.

For each of the three routines below, choose one thing that is really meaningful to you.

1. Self-reflection (talking to yourself about what you want in life: affirmations, mindfulness meditation, yoga, visualization, etc.)

2. Exercise (speed walking, biking, brisk dog-walking, tai chi, etc.)

3. Creativity (writing, music, sculpture, etc.)

4. Volunteering (volunteering at local organizations, helping neighbours, etc.)

These will be the starting point for your daily routine. It's OK if they change over time and I usually suggest you start with numbers one to three and only add number four after about six months; however, some people do start with all four from day one. It's up to you. Do what feels right and what will inspire you to get at it six days a week.

The next steps in your daily routine:

- Choose one day of the week to be your day off.
- Start with five to 15 minutes of each exercise per day, six days of the week.
- Keep a daily chart of how much time you do in each part of your daily practice. When you don't get to do that amount of time on one or more days, go over your notes judgment-free and figure out what threw you off your routine. From this, determine your own way to minimize your distractions and strengthen your commitment.
- Increase your time by about 20% a month until you end up with a daily routine that takes from one to two hours.
- Try using the following chart on a daily basis to fill in your work. Change the tasks to whatever your choices are. You can download a copy at:

http://www.reallifecoaching.ca/RealLifeCoaching/Success_Journal.html

The great thing about routines is that if they are connected to things you are passionate about, they will teach you the power there is in working daily on things you love. If you are only partially passionate about them, pretend to be passionate and pretty soon you will be.

A young man of 19 years (let's call him Thomas) e-mailed me one day claiming that he felt helpless about overcoming his procrastination. Thomas had done well at a fiercely academic private high school, but was completely unprepared for the danger that the freedom of university would bring. He had called me after having barely survived his first year in university.

Nothing had worked to motivate him. His lack of oversight to do the required studying for his classes had incapacitated him and he was unable to do what he needed to do in the final crunch. Having barely survived and faced with the upcoming year, Thomas confided to me that "I've tried many times before and failed, so I'm wondering if I try again, why would I succeed this time?" His feelings of powerlessness, of not trusting himself to get things done was both stressful and depressing for him. "So, I think I need some help. Plenty more details if you think you could help."

Before calling me, Thomas had already organized a budget of what he could afford in terms of professional coaching. In June, he had analyzed and selected his next semester's courses, chosen for their ability to get his science credits done while avoiding the math "issues" he had. In

Daily Routine www.realifecoaching.ca								
Week Of:	Date:					Your name here		
Task	Minutes	M	T	W	Th	F	S	S
Self-Reflection								
Exercise								
Creative								
Volunteering								
Option "v" for checkmark	Affirmation							

great detail, based on his first year's experience, Thomas had graded and summed up many of the challenges he might face in the coming year.

I responded the following morning saying that I really appreciated his candour and that I knew that I could help him if he was willing to try something a little different. Over the next few weeks of Skype sessions, I learned that Thomas had felt like a "lone wolf" in high school. He had his own way of doing things and when it came to tests and reports, he would only bother doing the parts worth "big points" and knock them out of the park. Getting 80s and 90s in these well-chosen targets, allowed him to end up with good grades while still getting in lots and lots of gaming time.

University had been a rude awakening. He had found that all his "just-in-time" approaches did not work. To make matters worse, he spent more and more time at the bars trying to make new friends and found the only way to overcome his shyness was to drink more and more alcohol.

So, there were three aspects that we had to change quickly:

1. A simple daily routine to start feeling a bit in control of himself.
2. A drinking schedule to get some handle of his out-of-control ways.
3. A starting regimen for studying.

1. The Simple Daily Routine

Upon personal reflection, he told me it was clear that what he was saying to himself on a regular basis was self-defeating. "As soon as I think about giving up then I'm bound to give up, so it's already too late." He was a harsh judge of himself and we had to change his focus away from what "stopping" looked like and move it toward what brought him to university in the first place—his enjoyment of the subjects that interested and challenged him. We ended up with the following affirmation: "I am going to pursue a good academic base for the year. This is my main goal." He was to repeat this for five minutes in the morning and five minutes in the evening. This was emotionally routed in a success he had had earlier in his life winning a chess tournament. He remembered how he felt when he had won; he remembered the sound of people cheering, the feeling in his heart of happiness, and the relief that it was over and that he had won. I had him relive those positive feelings as he repeated the affirmation.

His daily exercise was to go for a walk around the campus without his phone or music. His creative exercise was to write a series of science fiction short stories, emphasizing the love that brought him to science in the first place.

2. The Drinking Schedule to Gain Control

We decided that he would limit his drinking to two "pre-drinks" followed by one drink at the clubs. Instead of going out five nights a week, he would try living with three.

3. The Study Regimen

We found that we had to include a study schedule as he had basically put in zero time in the previous year. We came up with four 30-minute sections a day, six days a week. He found that he had difficulty doing 30 minutes straight. So we ended up with a plan of two groups of five ten-minute units with a two-minute break in between each unit. I suggested that once this habit became solid, he try increasing the units by increments of two minutes (from 10 to 12, from 12 to 14 etc., until he reached our original four 30-minute sections.) If he felt overwhelmed as he was increasing, he could just go back to the last successful increment and stay there for a few more days then try increasing again.

When we next met, Thomas showed me the weekly schedule we had set up with his times written in. The two days we met (Monday and Thursday), he had done all of his routines. The following days (Tuesday and Friday), he had done half the work, and by the third day (Wednesday and Saturday), he had done little if any of his work.

I pointed out the pattern and told him that it showed that he had done well on his own the day following our session. I asked him what had motivated him to do his work that day. He told me that the affirmation had helped him. I suggested that the "echo day," the third days—Wednesdays and Saturdays—were the ones he would have to make a conscious choice to be in charge of.

This system worked for him and he began increasing his study load and getting in control of his shyness-based drinking habits. He has told me that he feels he finally has a frame that he can grow on so when he begins to feel that he isn't doing enough and he might as well give up, he just looks at his weekly time sheets and sees his progress and soldiers on.

His confidence has been growing, attracting people to him, and he has met some great new friends on his walks around campus. He is now ready for Step Five.

"Each moment of the day makes or unmakes character."

~ Oscar Wilde ~

Step Five

Out into the World

If you were to ask a young person in their teens or twenties where they really love to be, they would say without hesitation: "I love being in my room!" That room connects them to all the things they enjoy: video gaming, rpg-ing, texting, and whatever new way to "spend" time the world comes out with. Their room has become, in effect, a "box of safety;" this is both a good thing and a bad thing. The bad thing about the box of safety is that everything and everywhere else is not their box of safety, making the "unboxed world" feel a little like the universe outside Doctor Who's telephone booth when it is whirling around. The good thing about the box of safety is that they have at least one place where they really feel safe. Once someone feels safe in one place, there is the possibility to get them to feel safe in other places.

The question becomes: How do you make the unboxed world into a box of safety? And the answer is: You don't! You create portable "boxes of safety," one at a time until there are more safe places than unsafe places and eventually you can make any place safe-(ish).

The following exercise is to help create portable "boxes of safety" out there in the r/w (real world). If you have followed the past four Steps laid out in this book, you have already begun to develop the strengths and successes that come from having a personal daily routine.

The challenges now are:

1. Taking this personal routine out into the world.
2. Interacting with others in empowered ways.
3. Keeping the daily routine going while dealing with new distractions as well as new work that may come your way from volunteering and/or hobbies "out there."
4. Engaging that world successfully and safely.

(whew!)

I strongly suggest to anyone trying this next step that it include one or both of the following: hobbies and volunteering. By hobbies, I would suggest generative ones: music, dancing, martial arts, a book club, comedy troupes, etc. By volunteering, I suggest you try one of the following: helping people less fortunate than yourself or working in an area that you are interested in but don't have the necessary credentials or experience to get "a real job" in.

Generative Hobbies

Join a group engaged in your generative hobby (not magic cards, etc.) and commit to being there once or twice a week. Make sure the schedule is one you can do successfully on an ongoing basis. Find out what is required of you (in music, for example, you'll have to know the music well enough to hold your own in performing the songs) and how much time you would need to invest at home daily (15 to 30 minutes is a good amount of time in general).

Volunteering

Volunteering as an act of giving: do some research on local groups that help people in a way that you find meaningful. Look for places that give some sort of training. One volunteer group I know of gave their volunteers a fantastic course on Active Listening which I strongly recommend.

Volunteering as an apprenticeship: there are so many wrong ways to volunteer in for-profit organizations. The secret to volunteering successfully is to:

- Choose an area that truly fascinates you and that you would consider as a vocation.
- Find out the interests of the people with whom you will be speaking.

- Be sure to think about what you can bring to your volunteer position and what benefit they will get from it.
- If they act like they are doing you a favour—don't go there!
- Add the following disciplines to your daily routines and you will find yourself strengthening your old skills, and adding new ones:
- Be consistent.
- Do your best even when you don't feel like it and the novelty has worn off.
- Deal with challenging people and deal with engaging people. Dealing with either can throw you off.
- Keep to your daily routine when things get a little nuts "out there."

Now take the following and add it to your daily routine sheet. Put in the time you spend at your new weekly "outings," and add in your travelling time as well as any home time you require to practice or read.

You are now mixing your home base of success with the opportunities "out there." Your challenge is to not let the unexpected throw you off your daily routine. More than likely, it will from time to time, but when it does throw you off, start back with your basics—self-reflection, exercise, and creativity. Choose whichever basic trait is easiest for you to start up with at the moment. Eventually you will get back on that horse and ride, baby, ride!

This becomes your hero's journey; your adventure out into the real world. This is your portable box of safety, the one you build by growing character and doing what is required one day at a time. By the way, it really does feel great (but don't let it get around).

"A man practices the art of adventure when he breaks the chain of routine and renews his life through reading new books, traveling to new places, making new friends, taking up new hobbies and adopting new viewpoints.

~ Wilfred Peterson ~

Step Six

How to Arrest Your Time Stealers

So here you are. If you have been following this system you have:

1. Assessed your strengths and challenges.

2. Found a mentor, selected goals, and identified ways of confirming success.

3. Looked at the inner blocks that were preventing you from achieving and began implementing the appropriate changes to free yourself from those blocks.

4. Created a daily routine of positive exercises to mentally nourish and strengthen yourself.

5. Gone out into the world and started meeting people and working on your interests.

Now meet your greatest challenger. The time stealer. He (or she) is fun, charming, and great to be with, someone you are happy to do things with, gets all your jokes, and is just all around great to kill time with.

Yes, the time stealer is a time killer. You can never get back the lost time; still, you value the time spent with them. Who are they? What are their names? They are called: friend, video games, T.V., the Internet, texting, tweeting, twitting, (feel free to fill in the rest... with your spare time).

What? But they have so many good qualities! You value your time with them. Being without them would suck. Big time! ....I couldn't agree with you more.

No one should be punished for spending time with their time stealers. We should value the time we spend with these stealers, but time not measured is time badly spent.

So, this Step is about giving all of your wants and needs a time and space in moderation.

Do stuff first!

How many times have you said: if I just do "A," then I'll do my "B." But when sleep-time comes around, and you haven't gotten to "B" 'cuz you got lost in "A"...what do you do? Don't sweat it! Just resolve to do your daily routine things next time (and that includes work for your day gig, as well) then give time to your time stealer(s). If that seems too much of "A" before you get to "B," then see if you are able to work in 10, 20, or 30-minute blocks with a five or 10-minute break as a reward between each block. You might consider putting on a timer for the break time so that you keep to it. This is a great help to a lot of my clients and, as they improve, they find they can work for longer periods and enjoy the deeper levels of concentration that they get to.

Stealers don't give up easily

Time stealers like you. They know you appreciate them and so they want to "help" you see more of them. But hey! What are limits to friends? Limits? We don't need no blinkin' limits! All of a sudden, there is a weekend long magic card event for the new deck or the best RPG ever comes out and you get to beta-test...

You get the picture and you know it always happens just when you decide to get serious.

Go for it! That's right. Do it but decide not to do the whole weekend but maybe a few hours.

Abstaining from your time stealers means that your sub-conscious will find a way to trip you up, mess up your good stuff, and have you decide: "Well, that didn't work! I might as well go back to the stealers."

Use your time stealers as a reward: If I do "x" amount of "y" then I can go play "z"!!

What do you do when your time stealers are your hangout buddies?

Setting limits is about giving people what they want at a time when it is good for both of you. Making your daily routine time unavailable to others is easy. Let me tell you about a friend and co-worker of mine named Veronica from the seven years that I taught middle school.

Veronica and I were putting together an end-of-year concert with 500 students, 300 of hers (J.K to grade four) and 200 of mine (grades five to eight). We would have them do the first and last songs together and I would be conducting the 500 (as they were my arrangements of the songs).

The deadline loomed large upon us and, as we looked for rehearsal times, certain times were just unavailable to us. We found the right ones. The rehearsals went well (I don't know if you can imagine what it's like to get an entire school to sing together :-O) and the show was a big success.

In the months following the concert as I got to know Veronica, I realized that some of those unavailable times were her times to work out. She was in healthy shape and she kept herself that way by making her training time sacred. She didn't need to explain it to me. She just told me that she wasn't available at those times.

Use Veronica's example and block off your time. Tell your friends that you are available at a certain time and get them and your family used to the fact that when you are doing your work, you are not available.

Killing ourselves with kindness

One of the easiest ways to end up wasting time is because we thought our friends would feel bad if we didn't always make ourselves available to them when they were free. Friends are so important, but good friends want to see you achieve. Most of the time, they will be fine with a slightly different get-together time. Find out if it is ok. It usually is.

We sacrifice our time for people because of what we assume is important to them… Don't assume. Ask!

And now, meet the biggest time stealer you will ever meet in your life: you. That's right. You are your biggest challenge. Not friends, or the computer, or anything else. You have to decide on a purpose. It really doesn't matter if it's the right one. You can change it every month or every year, whenever you have found something better, but start right now!

Decide to make your time "on purpose." Make sure you are always connected to what your purpose is and if something doesn't suit your purpose, put it aside for a bit. Set goals and don't let too much time drift away until those goals can be ticked off as done.

"Dost thou love life?
Then do not squander time, for, that's the stuff life is made of."
~ Benjamin Franklin ~

Step Seven

Direction—Following Your Bliss

What if you could do anything you wanted to with your life?

What would you do? How would you be? How would you go about it? Who would you seek out? What if what you went after wasn't what you thought it would be? How would you know when you'd arrived?

Be careful for what you wish for. I am going to give you the tools to make whatever you want to have happen happen. For long-term success, ensure that what you do will be of benefit to all whom your happenings touch. These tools have been shared many times in many ways by many people, but these are written for you. Just make sure what you wish for is what you truly want.

- **Pick your target:** What is it that makes you happy when you are doing it but also contributes to the human collective? If this is something that would bring you joy in doing for the next ten years, then choose this as your target.

- **Be the arrow:** The only thing stopping us is our fears and our limiting beliefs. When we eliminate those, anything is possible. If you have reached this Stage in the Steps to success, you are ready to go after your dreams. Don't let anyone tell you they are impractical. Don't let anyone tell you, you can't reach them. The people who have achieved greatness had everything you and I have, but they also had the conviction to follow their bliss.

The Bliss Process

- **Target:** Think of your target. Make it your focus for everything you do from now on. As you get closer to your target, you will receive tempting offers to do other things. If it is not "on target," let it go! You will be richly rewarded for staying true.

- **Aim:** The short-term method for hitting your target requires aim. Focus on what you need to do to hit your target and make this your daily focus.

- **Adjust:** Nothing comes easy (unless you truly believe it can). When you aim and miss, be okay with missing, then simply adjust, re-aim, and do it again. Someone once said: "I'm either getting it right or I'm learning."

- **Seek out those like-minded:** If you are the smartest and anything-est in your group, find another group. Your life skills are affected by those with whom you spend time. If they are successful and happy, you will learn subtle skills and a positive subconscious self-speak. This positive self-speak will propel you towards success, bringing you joy and happiness through association. Great people have the unique ability of making us think we can be great.

- **Reboot the arrow:** People never die regretting what they did; they die regretting what they didn't do. Having said that, sometimes you dive into something, embrace it with all of your heart only to discover it wasn't for you. Here, you have two schools of thought: those who say "you started it, you finish it or you're a quitter," and those who say "life is a series of experiences bumping into accidents on the way to your bliss." I agree with the latter; it's not what you do but what you learn from the experience that counts.

- **Pierce the target:** Guess what, we almost never arrive. Once you are on your true path, new targets will arise and new adventures will unfold themselves. It is only in trying to make the world a bit better that we leave a legacy of love that resonates beyond the ages. Nothing resonates as much as loving your fellow human being. So many people spend their lives looking at what is wrong with the world. Look for what is right. It's easier and more fun.

Abraham was coming for his first session and I had asked him what his goals were: he said that he wanted to get along with his family (he lived with his aunt and uncle), get physically healthy, and have a great job. These were great goals for anyone, but Abraham was someone considered by others to have a low probability of success in life on his own. Years of testing had convinced all those around him that he had impenetrable challenges in communication and organization.

However, in our work together, I discovered that Abraham simply tested badly and was very much in need of a different approach to learning how to communicate and organize.

I asked Abraham what he thought were his obstacles to his goals. He said that when it came to getting along with this family, he was either at a loss for words, didn't know how to use the words he had, or just said things that he would later regret.

When we got to his indicators of success, he said that success would be when he could have a conversation with his uncle where they didn't end up shouting and he didn't end up being told that he couldn't be trusted.

As an exercise, I had him take one of my articles, read it on his own, and then come back to me with his own explanation. At the next session, Abraham came in and avoided eye contact with me from the moment I greeted him at the door.

When we sat down, I asked how his week went and he said that he had told his uncle what we were going to do and his uncle had taken his hand and told him not to expect too much of himself, that they both knew he couldn't do it. He was just a lousy communicator.

I asked him: "Abraham, what would it feel like to become a good communicator?"

He stammered. "I–I don't have the words. I'm a lousy talker."

"Take your time, Abraham. Take your time. I can wait."

"I want to feel like… like there's this race and all these people are cheering me and I'm almost at the finish line. And I'm first!" he continued.

"How does that feel Abraham?"

"Good," he said.

"Powerful?"

"Powerful!" he exclaimed.

I asked him: "Abraham, what stops you from being powerful?"

You could see the wheels turning and turning in his head and after what seemed like a very long time, he said; "It's like… (he frowned and his head dropped) I don't know the words."

"Abraham, say it any way you want. You're in charge here. You call the shots."

He sighed. "It's like there's this ball and there's this boy… and the ball's on that side of the fence and the boy is on this side of the fence. And if he goes there, the ball's not there anymore. His parents are just watching from the window. Not doing anything. Just watching. And I want to tell him… I want to tell him…"

"Tell him what, Abraham?"

Abraham continued: "I want to tell him, the ball's already on your side. You just gotta believe."

He looked up at me nervously, not knowing what I would say. I smiled and said: "Abraham, you know how you said that you're a lousy talker. A lousy communicator? You're one of the best communicators I've ever met."

I showed him his words in print on the screen. These beautiful, meaningful words he had just said. This light shone on his face and he beamed. He beamed with pride and joy.

"I said that?" he asked in shock.

"Yes Abraham."

"I said that!" he shouted.

"What does that make you Abraham?" I asked.

After a long thoughtful pause he mumbled: "I dunno."

"A good… what?" I coached.

"A good… communicator?" he said tentatively.

"Yes! A great communicator!" I exclaimed. Abraham, you speak like poetry. I believe you think like poetry. That's why no one gets you yet. You're too hip for them! Once you believe in the beautiful way that you see things, I'll show you how you can make it boring enough so that regular people can understand what you see. But Abraham, keep the poetry. It's like your superpower. If you were a superhero, Abraham, which one would you be?

He dropped his head and said: "I'd probably be Clark Kent."

"Abraham, the way you see things. I know…. you're Superman. Do you know why Superman has to be Clark Kent?"

He looked up at me, puzzled: "No."

"Because the world's not ready for Superman in everyday life. They can't handle it, so Superman ends up being Clark Kent. Maybe when you believe in this talent… this amazing talent you have you have to communicate and learn to make it boring for people, they'll start listening. Then one day they'll be ready for the Superman in you."

I guess what I saw in Abraham is what I see everyday—that in each person there's a hero, going on a hero's journey. Very often they're disguised as slackers, fumblers, failures, pranksters just trying to protect themselves. Feeling in danger practically every moment of their lives, they hide their true powers, powers they may not yet believe in. But here's the thing: we also have a power. Each and every one of us, if we choose to… can help another person let their powers shine.

How do you do that? How do we all do that? By seeing the Superman in Clark Kent.

"What did you do as a child that created timelessness that made you forget time? Therein lies the myth to live by."

~ Joseph Campbell ~

Stage Two
Professional Development

You can study, you can practice, you can philosophize all you want, but it means diddly until you test it out there in the "real world." By following the previous steps to success in Stage One you have transformed yourself into someone who can move beyond your safety zone. You are now learning to seek out what makes you happy in a disciplined, organized way with proper support from mentors, friends, and family. Professional development is about taking this new inner confidence and testing it against the different challenges that come from an unknown and uncertain world. The best way to do that is in small manageable steps. The next step for someone searching to find success "out there" is to put three toes in the water.

Step Eight

Three Toes in the Water

Why three toes? If you do one thing and it works (or doesn't), it could just be "luck." Either way, keep going. If you do two things successfully, it can still be an anomaly. If you do three things well, you now have a pattern. True, naysayers can poop on pretty much anything, but if you get three consecutive successes, I say: "Yahoo!" If you get three straight failures, remember that Edison took 10,000 wrong tries to find the right filament. It was that perseverance that created the incandescent bulb.

Picking a new pond to swim in:

Choose: university, college, business, or a fourth choice. Create a three-month challenge and bring your recent successes into a new "real life" situation. You can do almost anything if you do it with passion and are willing to slog through the occasional grinding that accompanies learning any skill, course, or trade.

University or College:

Pick a subject that you would love to learn more about, something you could see yourself doing for the next ten years and liking it. Go to three schools in your area, get their syllabus, meet with the registrar, and pick three classes—two core-related and one bird class to test your learning chops on.

Entrepreneur:

Pick something you love doing. See who makes a living selling that product or service. Go volunteer to work there for a 12-week period. It might be in sales, or promotions, or as a stock-boy, but make sure you know where you want to be at the end of the 12 weeks.

Something else:

A lot of your passions may not seem easy to make a living at (isn't that what a lot of parents tell us?) but chances are someone figured out a way to make a living at it. Find out who did and if it can be repeated or modified to your own way of doing things. See if you can find people who have made a living at it in your area and apprentice with them.

Read:

How to Win Friends and Influence People by Dale Carnegie (*HTWFAIP*). This is the best book I found to teach the basic skills on how to "sell" yourself and to get people to want to help you by showing them that you are genuinely interested in them.

Recap:

Pick three subjects of interest for one semester or a 12-week mentorship and use the tools for success to do the work (and homework) required. Find people who are passionate about that pond and get to know them. **You can learn so much from passionate people who succeed.**

One of the most important tips I could ever give you...

Secretaries hold the keys!

Always be respectful of the people you first get in contact with wherever you go. Very often, these people know the right person for the right task in their domain and they can get you there. Take a moment to learn their names, use them in a natural way two or three times in the conversation; find out why they chose to work there and what they like about it.

Avoid interrogating!

Listening is the best way to converse. However, as "the lost chapter" in *HTWFAIP* taught us, there are some people who are just plain never going to give you the time of day or be kind. So, don't be shy. If you are not getting anywhere, respectfully ask to see a more senior person. Sometimes that is enough to get the front line person to help you, sometimes it gets you to the next level. Don't forget to enjoy the pond. It's new and you benefit by embracing every opportunity to grow. May the three toes guide your steps to adventure!

Well, you'll be happy to know that Skeeter made it to Stage Two—Professional Development. His addictions no longer had the hold on him that they used to. He had proved himself "out there" and now it was time to put three toes in the water. (I wonder where he kept the other toes.)

Through a long process of self-reflection, research, and meeting with people in different fields, Skeeter chose biology. This required one biology course, Principles of Cell Biology; a bird course, Introductory to Anthropology (he heard it was a great place to meet girls); and the dreaded math-beast, Calculus (Skeeter's kryptonite).

Skeeter's *HTWFAIP* skills came in very handy in inspiring the registrar person to help him get the best course but math is math (sigh).

Skeeter continued to do his self-reflection, walking, and guitar playing (his daily routine), and added a 2:1 ratio of studying (hypothetically). His nine hours of class meant he would do three hours a day of study, broken into 30-minute segments.

He also made some great non-stoner friends (something new for him) and found it felt good being around people who were successful at what they did.

He mixed up the stuff he hated with the stuff he felt good about and all was great… until the new RPG came out. It had been years in the making. Skeeter had loved the previous incarnation of the franchise and he was sure that one "lost weekend" of gaming couldn't be a bad thing. Well, it came a week before mid-terms and the lost weekend became a lost ten days.

Skeeter barely passed anthropology, did ok-ish in cell biology, and failed math. In his last two run-ins with university, this was the point where he would bow out of school without it affecting his permanent record; but this was Skeeter 2.0 and he had no intention of giving up. He has seen through all the previous work we had done together that he could do things on his own steam; messing up did not mean having to give up.

The first thing he did was to dismantle his video box and he gave it to his Dad and told him to put it somewhere where Skeeter would never see it. He then committed to texting me every time he completed a 30-minute practice session for the first week. Acknowledging his accomplishments allowed him feel some accountability again.

He found someone who offered the previous year's tests for math and got him to tutor him. The big difference was that he refused to be spoon-fed by the tutor. He would do the problems and then ask for help from the tutor to increase his speed and get clarity on the stuff he didn't get.

Skeeter ended up getting an 80% average on his three classes by the end of the term and it was all on his own steam. He also played the heck out of that RPG during the break and he totally earned it!

> *"If I have ever made any valuable discoveries, it has been owing more to patient attention than to any other talent."*

> ### ~ Sir Isaac Newton ~

Step Nine

Feeling Safe "Out There"

> **Warning to new parents!**
>
> **Set up your children's computer and play systems in a communal room. Leave them their bedroom for books and music.**

Now for the gazillion people who haven't done that… the following is for you.

Once upon a time the idea of kids doing homework in their bedroom seemed like a good idea: they would have privacy, quiet, and fewer distractions. When computers appeared on the scene and became affordable, you naturally thought: why not put one in the bedroom so little Skeeter would have access to… does anyone remember what computers did before they do what they do? When the new-fangled game attached to the TV called *Pong* was replaced by more and more sophisticated computer games, a whole can of virtual worms opened up.

Well, here we are in the new millennium standing at the inner sanctum formerly known as "bedroom." Could people ever have imagined such a cool place becoming a reality, when the "fortress of solitude" used to be a snow castle and *The Ed Sullivan Show* was watched in the parent's bedroom on a 19" TV, with older sisters screaming into the ears of anyone within a five-mile radius as The Beatles sung *She Loves You?*

In Step Eight, I suggested that you create a 12-week test period: one term at school or at an apprenticeship that would use your success skills of 1) daily routine, 2) discipline, and 3) following your positive passions.

If you have started this process, you now are stuck in the middle of "out there" without your inner sanctum. Now, I want to introduce you to a way that works to create new and positive safety zones.

The difference between boxes of safety and zones of safety

Your bedroom has been a box of safety with sides, a top, and a bottom. When you first ventured out into the world in Stage One, you were recreating portable boxes of safety. These portable boxes work really well in static, short-term experiments, but the real world is fluid and we want you to feel safe anywhere, anytime, in any circumstance. For this, you will require a zone of safety. This is a moveable area that surrounds you and allows you to traverse the world, free of anxiety, free of fear, and free of everything your parents told you or implied would be scary. It is what you bring within you that will make it safe. To create the inner safety that will build outer zones of safety, we need to incorporate certain new variations in our habits.

Everybody has habits. Some help you and some keep you stuck. We choose our habits to create small cozy places of safety. But often these cozy places do not allow us to grow. They stop us from feeling the power of success through challenges and keep us in our place.

Transforming your negative zones into positive ones

If you went out into the world and it didn't go so well the first time, you may have subconsciously created negative zones of safety, using your "bad habits" to help connect you with people of similar habits. These zones do make you feel safe-ish by surrounding yourself with people who live like you and "get" your lifestyle, but there is a price to pay for those particular zones of safety.

What did you do to create your negative safety zones? Did you use your most efficient negative habits to great effect? Did you hang with fellow World of Warcrafters or play at the local magic card shop? When you went out into the world, perhaps to the first college/university that you almost flunked out of, did you look for smokers, for stoners? Guess what? You had the perfect skills to find warm cozy zones of safety. You had the buzz words, the affectations—bleary eyes, stubble, video game t-shirts, etc.—to gain instant access to these cozy zones. They made anywhere you went a safe place... overall. This is how one grinds their negative habits into negative zones of safety. They work but they don't get you anywhere worthwhile.

The same system works to create positive safety zones. Positive safety zones have different buzz words and affectations—being passionate about your work, showering regularly, knowing your work, arriving prepared, making your word your bond, and most importantly, acting as if you believe in yourself.

So with your new all-access pass, you can more easily find common ground with students/co-workers, hang with the people who stay late or get in early, talk to the prof/manager/boss. You are now ready to talk to the T.A's or secretaries and I encourage you to do so. Write this following statement and put it somewhere that you will see it first thing in the morning and last thing at night: ***Your prime task is to find the people who are also "on purpose."*** It doesn't matter what their purpose is; it matters that they are following their bliss. Remember: if the new friends/classmates/teachers do not fit your purpose, find others who do.

You are now in a new and positive safety zone, meeting with people who will accept you for following your purpose and who share your qualities of passion and determination. Eventually, it will feel just as good as the old zones, but you will perceive something new entering your consciousness… the glimmer of hope that you may find greatness in your life and rise up to make it happen. At this point, each positive action builds upon itself, every setback becomes merely a minor bump on the road you are travelling on, and everything leads you towards your bliss.

It's easy for someone else to preach to you how to be in a new envionment but for most people, the unknown can seem kind of scary. It's hard to figure out how to "act," no matter what others say. Here are some tips on how to make these new situations successful.

Some tips on getting good stuff in new safety zones

1. Imagine a person who inspires you: real, fictional, or from the past. Someone who has a quality that would be perfect to inhabit for a particular situation.
   a. Imagine them being there "in your shoes."
   b. How would they walk into the room?
   c. How would they sit, stand, and comport themselves?
   d. What would their presence be like?

Enter your new zone with these qualities and try the following:

1. Listen to the people you meet as if you are your inspiring character.
2. Avoid telling rambling stories. It trains people to tune you out.
3. Encourage people to talk about themselves and validate the things

to which you relate.

4. Ask questions about the parts of what they are saying that you may not know much about and be open to learning something new.

5. Make your points or ideas and then make sure you give the other person a chance to comment or lead the conversation elsewhere.

6. Validate their points.

7. Give the impression of an ease of being there that indicates that you belong.

8. Be positive.

9. Say "yes!" (when appropriate).

Try different ways of acting in public in different situations. Pick the ones that suit you. These may change depending on different circumstances and mindsets. Use these opportunities to rise above your fears and if it doesn't go as you had hoped or it freaks you out and ends up being a 20 out of 10 on the suck-o-meter, try a new variation next time. Determine for yourself in advance that you will not give up after one bad situation.

Be willing to try anything worthwhile three times.

"If you want a quality, act as if you already have it. If you want to be courageous, act as if you were—and as you act and persevere in acting, so you tend to become."

~ Norman Vincent Peale ~

Step Ten

From Crud to Cred:
Creating New
Generative Structures

So here you are taking another stab at "making it" in life. Your parents are cautiously optimistic. You are non-committal. Your dog still thinks your amazing (but he likes Yanni). It should go well. You're older. You've faced your share of "challenges" and you've survived. You're not on the street or in a cult or both. Then why so nervous?

Well, there is the unpleasant memory of the last time you went out into the "real world" and it so didn't "work." Like if "work" was the bag you use to pick up crud, your experience would be the stuff that's stays on the ground where the crud was. (Not a good place unless you are a crud-worm.)

Now you have done all this personal growth. You have:

- Learned to create a daily program of positive things to do.
- Set limits on the time stealers in your life.
- Created goals and ways to reach those goals that were tried and tested.
- Built up a lot more faith in yourself then ever before...

But some part of you (the lizard/slacker brain known as "Lizzie") remembers what happened before when you were tested out in the real world but that part won't care about "progress" once you are out there. Lizzie is going to do her best to convince you that you really need to start a *Babylon V* retrospective the night before your begin your new classes or job. She may tell you that being late is fashionable or any number of things that will get you to give up before you have given yourself a good shot at it, because Lizzie's here to tell you that giving up keeps you safe.

I'm here to tell you that if you got this far and you are willing to give it another try for yourself… not for anyone else, you can do it! Simply follow these steps:

Ten Steps to Help Change Your Life from Crud to Cred(ability)

1. Create a daily schedule of things you do for you:
   - Meditation.
   - Walking (electronics-free).
   - Something creative.

2. Write down all the regular appointments you have:
   - Going to work/class.
   - Meetings.

3. Set up your study times:
   - Multiply your amount of class hours by your study factor, 1:1, 2:1, or 3:1.
   - Break them down by day and then by units. If you can do 25-minutes sessions with a five minute break in-between, make it so! But if you need a **different starting point that you can handle,** you can always begin with 10-minute sessions with two-minute breaks and build on them.

4. Figure out a good sleep schedule:
   - When to start getting ready for sleep.
   - When you want to be asleep (roughly).
   - When you need to wake up.
   - How much time you need before you are actually ready to get going or talk to people.

5. Don't promise what you won't do:
   - Sometimes is seems so much easier when your parents are nervous about you succeeding to humour them just to get them

off your case. This does help short term but ruins all your credibility long term. If they are on your case too often, choose a quiet time to listen to their concerns, say back to them what you heard in your own words and tell them what you are willing to do. Let them know that when they give you space, it helps you feel they believe in you and if they do give you the space, try to remember to show some appreciation.

6. Give more than what you are asked for:
    *   One parent recently told me his son is a minimalist. If he needs a 75, he gets a 75. If you want the front lawn mowed and there are some scraggly bushes on the side, if they weren't part of the bargain, they stay scraggly. Give more than you are asked for and you are putting positive will in your cred bank to be cashed in on a later date. The same goes for school.

7. Avoid negative slang:
    *   So many young people use derogatory words about other groups of people to say that things are odd or messed up. If you are using derogatory words, you never know who you might be unintentionally hurting.

8. Say "Yes!":
    *   It's so much easier to opt out of things and there is definitely a case for being taken advantage of but when it is reasonable and only takes a little extra time, offer your services to someone who asks.

9. Embrace appreciation:
    *   Notice the good things people do and let them know about it.

10. Embrace criticism:
    *   Not yours of them. Theirs of you. Useful criticism can help you look at parts of yourself that you might not have noticed, but remember to always consider the source.

So how do these things help you change your life from sucking to not sucking? By helping you focus on the very best of you. That way, it doesn't matter whether people notice or not. What's most important is that **you** know and that's all you need. Life is inevitable, sucking is optional.

A practical example

Let's say you're going to do the school thing à la Skeeter.

- You have four classes—three in your major and one elective.
- You've joined three clubs—salsa dancing, yoga, and debating—all meeting once a week.
- You still see your mentor once or twice a week—twice a week when things are shaky and once a week when things are running smoothly.
- You have travel time, study time, your daily routine, and the stuff that magically gets done when you live at home (cleaning, laundry, getting toothpaste off of stuff, etc.)

First, take your daily schedule and write out the classes and the club meetings. If there are tutorials or any times available to work on the classes, include those as well. Work out how much time it takes to get to your class and include a 20% fudge factor so that no matter what messes up, you are still there on time. If there are team meetings for your classes, write them in as well. In this instance, Skeeter lives on-campus and travel time is not an issue.

Hours	Mon	Tues	Wed	Thurs	Fri	Sat	Sun
09:00							
09:30							
10:00							
10:30			Bio Tutorial				
11:00							
11:30	Bio 103		Bio 103				
12:00							
12:30							
13:00							
13:30							
14:00							
14:30		PSYC 100		PSYC 100			
15:00							
15:30							
16:00		BIO LAB	BIO 102	BIO 130			
16:30	Salsa						
17:00							
17:30							
18:00							
18:30							
19:00				Debating			
19:30							
20:00			Yoga				
20:30							
21:00							
21:30							
22:00							
22:30							
23:00							
23:30							

Decide on a ratio of class time to study time. Some say 3:1 is ideal but if you are a born-again-slacker, anything over 1:1 is an improvement and I am a fan of starting at 2:1 if you will do it. Using whatever formula you have chosen:

- Put in your study times.
- Choose your mentoring times.
- Put in your sleep times and wake times. Remember to include the amount of time and stuff you do to get to sleep as well as for waking up.

Hours	Mon	Tues	Wed	Thurs	Fri	Sat	Sun
12:00	Sleep	Sleep	Sleep	Sleep	Sleep		Sleep
08:00							
09:00	Wake Up	Wake Up	Wake Up	Wake Up	Wake Up		Wake Up
09:30							
10:00	Study	Study					
10:30			Bio Tutorial	Study			
11:00					Study		
11:30	Bio 103		Bio 103				
12:00							Study
12:30							
13:00	Study	Study		Mentor			
13:30							Study
14:00			Study				
14:30	Mentor	PSYC 100		PSYC 100	Study		
15:00							
15:30							
16:00		BIO LAB	BIO 102	BIO 130			
16:30	Salsa						
17:00							
17:30							
18:00							
18:30		Study	Study				
19:00	Study			Debating			
19:30							
20:00			Yoga				
20:30				Study			
21:00							
21:30		Study	Study				
22:00	Study						
22:30							
23:00							
23:30		Meditation					

Now figure out what times you can incorporate in your daily schedule: the self-reflection, physical, and creative. I do sometimes suggest that the "giving back" component be put on the back burner until you have your routine down.

Now if you have to do laundry, cleaning, cooking, tech stuff, etc., add those to your list now.

Hours	Mon	Tues	Wed	Thurs	Fri	Sat	Sun
12:00	Sleep	Sleep	Sleep	Sleep	Sleep		Sleep
08:00							
09:00	Wake Up	Wake Up	Wake Up	Wake Up	Wake Up		Wake Up
09:30							
10:00	Study	Study					
10:30			Bio Tutorial	Study			
11:00					Study		
11:30	Bio 103		Bio 103				
12:00					Shopping		Study
12:30							
13:00	Study	Study		Mentor			
13:30							Study
14:00			Study				
14:30	Mentor	PSYC 100		PSYC 100	Study		
15:00							
15:30	Walk						
16:00		BIO LAB	BIO 102	BIO 130			
16:30	Salsa						
17:00							Creative Project
17:30							
18:00				Chill Time			
18:30		Study	Study				
19:00	Study			Debating	Campus Walk		Walk or Meditation
19:30		Laundry					
20:00			Yoga	Meditation	Creative Project		
20:30				Study			
21:00	Creative Project	Walk					
21:30		Study	Study				
22:00	Study						
22:30							
23:00							
23:30		Meditation					

If you have been following this system, you know that this next level of scheduling will give you something harder to describe: a strength that comes from really seeing what needs to be taken care of throughout each day of the week. Ticking them off is empowering; not freaking when you miss a part of the day or a whole day but learning what threw you off… is life-changing.

Things are less scary when they go from vague impossibilities (crud) to something you can see and handle (cred). Go for it! You will lose the crud and gain the cred.

Step Eleven

Making your Addictions Work for you:
The Freedom of University or A "Good Kid Gone Bad"

A client wrote to me that he was finding it practically impossible to succeed at University. Although Bob had done well academically through elementary, middle, and high school, he had found that the art of social intercourse eluded him (as had the other kind). At university, away from home and the influences that had kept him on the straight and narrow, Bob was determined to change his fate. He had read every book he could get his hands on about becoming a "pick up artist" and surmised that his paralyzing anxiety over socializing could be overcome through the transformative powers of alcohol: an elixir flowing with easy abundance in the dusty dorm-rooms of higher education.

It seemed every night was another party. Mondays, Thursdays, and Saturdays had great dance club events—not to mention the days in between. With a fire in his belly from three of four pre-drinks to gather up his courage, Bob would sally forth in search of coolness, acceptance, and the hope of proving his manhood.

It would be an understatement to say that towards the end of each evening and after a dozen drinks or so (hard to keep count at that point), Bob would end up with vague recollections of a series of public co-ed tongue tonsillectomies and nothing to show for his adventure but a hangover, a reticence to wake up for school or do homework, a rash of throat infections, and a hangover (didn't he already say that?).

Bob's addiction wasn't to the alcohol but to the imagined freedom he thought he attained and his belief that it would bring him the conquest he so desired. The other addiction was his fear of "missing out" by not being there.

When Bob and I first started working together, we began on Bob's challenges with school. After six weeks of re-organizing his work habits, we got to where Bob was doing well with the six-day routine we implemented to improve his study habits. The results had been dramatic. From a first year mid-50's average, Bob was now averaging an 88.

Perhaps, as a subconscious backlash to the "new Bob," he went out one weekend on Thursday, Friday, and Saturday nights and did some things he was less than proud of—mainly a string or drunken tirades on the futility of "gettin' some" in this unfriendly world. With that past weekend in mind, we established that his "best booze days" were the Thursday and Saturday night parties. At this point, he was willing to limit himself to those events. As I saw him on Mondays and Thursdays, I suggested on this particular Monday that he commit to being booze-free until our Thursday meeting. This was going to be an intensive week of classes and he wanted to continue his new high-mark streak.

On Thursday, I suggested that he try not to go out again until we spoke on Monday. Since Friday would be his day for extra-curricular courses, it would be a great opportunity to do some good things in the evening where there would be girls and everyone would be sober.

Monday came around and Bob found that his Friday had been the best ever by having not gone out that Thursday night. He joined three interesting extra-curricular courses and he also committed to having only one or two pre-drinks, allowing himself to make better decisions, and bringing only enough money for three additional drinks. Bob used a giant cognac glass to save the money that came from minimizing his drinking out and with it, he bought an amazing new video game. As I write this, Bob rarely goes out to bars and has met a great girl who loves biology ☺.

Almost everyone you know is addicted to something. Whether their addiction is coffee, helping too much, jogging with shin splints, or something less socially acceptable, addictions are a way of life for many people.

For some, addictions limit their enjoyment of life and limit their successes in life as well. Many people simply have addictive natures whereas others can try the most addictive things and then say "Meh" and never do them again. The scary part is that until you know which one you are and which thing will be your "it" attraction, you never know what you are getting into or where it may lead.

The young clients I work with tend to be addicted to video gaming, magic cards, junk food, and/or cannabis. Many would say that their addictions seem to provide a level of comfort… a buffer from an unsafe world. It only becomes problematic when it rules your life. It doesn't really matter if the addiction is deemed "good for you" or "bad for you." **Something that rules your life has a different agenda than your higher intentions will have for you.**

Having an addictive nature means that you have a passionate nature. **So, how do you take these passions and make them become something generative, something that improves your quality of life?**

The Good Stuff

The following are the basics of the work I do with struggling teens and young adults with the goal of empowering them to take charge of their lives, loosening the hold that their addictions have on them.

- First, find your personal power by starting a daily routine that includes inner reflection, walking, something creative, and giving back to the world.
  - Chart it.
  - Own it.
  - Rise above the obstacles that stop you from doing it on a daily basis.
- Pretty soon, you will be in control of your private world and you will find that these successes give you a sense of self-worth that is truly empowering.

Using the Bad Stuff for the Good Stuff

When you still feel the urge to indulge, use it as a reward for doing the work you need to get done. If you can handle it, give yourself micro-rewards (10 minutes of Angry Birds for every 20 minutes of daily routine). Slowly increase the "work" time and reduce the "treat" time.

> ### Important
> The rewards should not impede your ability to get back to your routine. Certain addictions will not work with this system. If this does not work for you, establish all the things you need to get done in the day, then give yourself your indulging reward at the end of the routine.

If you are getting the rest of the day off once you've done your chores, try introducing a small segment of healthy stuff to do in your goofing off period. For example, do all of your daily work, your home work, and your daily routine, then go off and play video games until your head explodes (not literally please). At some point, when you are almost lost in your video game haze, choose to take a break and go and do 15 minutes of your "good stuff" once more. Just this small step will put you in charge of your passions. It's not easy but it is transformative. These exercises will work for those of you who can moderate with a bit of direction.

So what if you are not a moderator? What if you feel it seems impossible to do just a little bit of your passion addiction after doing what you were supposed to do? Then you proceed to one of the turkey aisles: lukewarm, cool, or cold and this cold turkey does not come with mayo.

Lukewarm means you can stop for the week, get your stuff done, and then go nuts on Magic card nights/weekend tournaments or whatever else burns away your time.

Cool means that you can stop for a period of a few months, get what you need to get done, and then start up again on vacations, giving yourself a week or so of turkey-free acclimation to get back to your real stuff once again.

But for some, you need that turkey chilled to the bone.

Cold means that once it is gone, it needs to stay gone because when you start up "that" addiction you cannot stop. In that case, if you can stop, stop for just that day, then the next day, then keep that stopping up… one day at a time.

There is another level of addiction where you may need outside intervention to help you stop whatever your addiction is. When what you do is truly self-destructive and you are losing yourself, your friends, your family, your employment, and possibly your life, go seek professional help and don't forget to pick the system that works best for you. You should still be in charge of what system you pick, but only if you have those moments of clarity to admit your problem and know what system will work "best for you," not necessarily "easiest for you."

Here's a bigger question about your guilty pleasures

Try to determine if these indulgences do or do not benefit you; if they don't benefit you, ask yourself: would I be better replacing them with something that brings out the best in me? Search for that thing that would be a worthy place for your passions, determine a plan of action, and change the world for the better.

Accept your passions, command them wisely, and vow to leave the world a slightly better place than before you came into it kicking and screaming.

"A man who has not passed through the inferno of his passions has never overcome them."

~ Carl Jung ~

Welcome
to
Stage Three

You may have begun following the Slacker's Guide system feeling like so many of my clients: coming from a place of great distress, feeling stuck, and unable to find a way through. Yet, by the time they had gone through the first two Stages, they found they had created a solid platform of self-awareness gained from rising above their challenges. This solid platform allowed them to propel themselves towards the third Stage: Inner Development. This is the place where you transform **your** life into a **rich** life; one that you can feel great about no matter what challenges come your way.

Step Twelve

Living a Full Life

Just imagine a happy, successful life where play-time is as fulfilling as work-time and learning-time. Relationships become opportunities for joy, sharing, and lots of close, meaningful contact that is mutually satisfying.

But seriously, we're talking about a full life for teens *and young adults.* Let's face it, those early years are not easy and they're not drama-free. Basically there's lots in them that sucks.

Know this: "You can have a full life that still sucks from time to time. You can have meltdowns and do some really dumb stuff. The difference being that, if you choose to, you can learn from it all."

Try the following exercises and share the experience with others. It could be a friend or a family member. The best way to really know something is: learn one, do one, teach one. You will be teaching the mindfulness exercises below.

Remember: Let the person you are sharing this work with learn through your example. Don't insist they try it but wait for them to ask to try some of it on their own; if they don't ask, wait for a time when they are going through a challenging moment and, after the dust settles, ask how mindfulness might have changed how they would have dealt with the situation.

Being mindful. We all have moments when we are at our best and nothing can throw us off. Sometimes it can feel like we are outside of ourselves watching the events take place and knowing what are the wise and just responses for anything that comes our way. That is being mindful. Then there are the times when we aren't so mindful; times when our antics get the 'rents to ask us: whose kid are you anyways?!?

What follows is a way to get yourself to be present and aware in all circumstances so that on your worst day, you are making conscious choices that can lead to great moments of clarity. I have been teaching this to young adults since 2001 and it always has met with success. Just know that sometimes it takes a bit more time to take hold. Don't give up. It really is worth it. If it was easy, everyone would do it.

It starts with quieting your mind at the beginning of a new day.

Take a few moments upon arising to breathe in slowly and deeply, and then let out the breath even more slowly. Try to focus, if you can, on the flow of your breath. Imagine letting go of any stress, tension, or worries and breathing in qualities such as calmness, peacefulness, or good health. Try doing this every day.

Taking a few moments to empty your mind "noise" can help you throughout the day perceive what is happening around you without your emotional filters getting in the way.

Repeat a meaningful phrase to yourself of something you wish to accomplish that day: i.e.

- Today, I will focus on being present for all conversations that are important to me and I will be great at it!
- Today, I am calm, centred, and open to being my best.
- Today, I will share my thoughts deeply, honestly, and with kindness.
- Today, I will be a team player, thinking about what will help us succeed.
- Make up your own here.

_____

_____

Now we shall bring this concept into our learning, work, play, and relationships.

Being mindful in learning

It doesn't matter if you are learning for school, work, or a hobby, being mindful is about seeing what learning style you are best at and how best to use it. Be aware of your strengths and use them to make your own successful ways grow.

- Take a moment and look at what you need to accomplish today in your learning.

- Break it down into sections and make a rough estimate of how much time is needed for each part.

- Figure out how much time is reasonable for you to prepare for today, taking into account the amount of study time at one-sitting, and how much break time is reasonable.

- Use your learning style: visual (V), auditory (A) or kinesthetic (K) and double-check their order of dominance for you. Adjust your learning so that you incorporate at least two styles in your work. For example if you are VAK, you might read the material, then repeat it aloud. If you are VKA, you might read it then write it in your own words, probably writing it out by hand would be best.

- When you are engaged in learning something, be aware of where your attention is and when it drifts, gently return it to the subject at hand.

Being mindful in work

There are constant opportunities at work to give more than what is requested of you. Each time you give a little more than what is asked of you from a caring, humble place, you set the forces of the law of return in motion. The law of return states that for every action, there is an equal or greater reaction. When you plant a seed and tend to it, you receive not just one seed back but a whole crop of whatever it was that you planted. If you are not rewarded when you have proven yourself, ask for that reward. If it is still not forthcoming, find some other employer who will appreciate your extra effort. Always give more than what is asked of you. You will get noticed for this and be rewarded over time, in one way or another.

Being mindful in play

There are so many aspects to being mindful at play. Not just in the details of the game but also in relating to the other players in the game. How do they present themselves? Will they be assets or liabilities? How are they when they win? How are they when they lose? What happens when something unexpected throws them off? This tells you so much more than just skill level can. More importantly, how are you in all those circumstances? Mindfulness in play is about being aware of the game, the people, and a sense of proportion while seeing the metaphors for how to be in life, in the act of play.

Being mindful in relationships

There are those who are always in some sort of a "relationship" and those who have never been in a relationship. If you are in a relationship, the two most important tools are:

- Learning to listen.
- Knowing how to argue well.

Learning to listen requires putting aside what you think is right and trying to understand things from your partner's perspective. Knowing how to argue well means focusing on what is annoying you at the time, without bringing in the past, judging, or blaming the person.

If you have not been in a relationship, you should know that one thing is for sure: nothing will get you to grow more than a serious relationship. It challenges all your comfort zones, takes away time from serious vegging, and offers so much in return.

Think of the type of partner you would want in your life. Think of their qualities and their demeanour, and then imagine the type of person you want to become to attract that person. This is still about being you but also about your growing to have a meaningful, mature relationship.

All of these different parts of being mindful make for a full life.

When you are mindful in these parts of your daily life, your life is one of being in the moment, of really living and not just killing time before going virtual. Learning to care and to matter may be one of the greatest assets you can attain because then your work, play, study, and relationships become places of experience—places of feeling, thinking, and growing.

Live each day like it was the only one you have. Care about people and learn from everything. Most importantly, write, blog, share stories and listen to stories because all we have after we're gone are the stories we leave behind. Leave a good one. Leave stories of a life lived on purpose that was well-lived and that touched others in a meaningful way. That is a full life. Maybe one day you will become the dreaded…. parent!

When parents embrace the idea that by living a full life, they can have a greater impact on their children than with all the words, all the images, and all the sounds running through a young person's life, they can truly change the world for the better.

Be the parent you always promised yourself you would be.

Step Thirteen

Helping Others Helps You

Most people feel something is missing in their lives. For many, there is an inner void that toys and money cannot fill. You could count your blessings (it worked for Ebenezer Scrooge). You are alive… you live in a country where you can vote, give an opinion, and live your life fairly free of obstructions. Still, sometimes that isn't enough for you to feel fulfilled. So, how do we bring meaning into our lives? How do we begin to feel truly alive? Do something crazy! Help someone.

Choose to make one small positive change in the world. Some will say it's a waste of time. Some will call you foolish. Let them. You are your own person. Don't do it for anyone else but yourself. Help someone up off the ground. Get them back on their feet. Do your thing. Slowly. Little by little. Put everything you have into it but don't tell anyone. Just do it.

> *"The antidote to discrimination and stigma*
> *is proximity and education."*
> *~ Dr. Catherine Zahn ~*

How do you do it?

1. **Choose:** Pick something you care about: homelessness, mental illness, discrimination, child poverty, elder abuse, etc. Make this your *passion mission.*

2. **Investigate:** Do research on it. Find out enough that you could talk to anyone about it for 10 minutes and make him or her want to join in and help.

3. **Discover:** Go visit three places that presently help people in your cause. Learn about it "in the flesh."

4. **Volunteer:** Volunteer once or twice a week at a place that represents your cause.

5. **Search for the single point:** Ask people in the know: what is the one thing that would help this group thrive?

6. **Communicate the single point:** Pick that positive point and go and talk about it with everyone who will listen.

7. **Find others:** Write down the names/contact information of the people who are moved by the idea.

8. **Invite others:** Set up a real or virtual meeting with all those people and decide on the one thing you want your politicians to change.

9. **Involve the larger community:** Talk to local politicians and ask them what is required to make that change happen and if they would endorse it. Find out what level of government can help.

10. **Make it an issue:** Use all that you have learned to make this a platform for change in upcoming elections at the proper level.

11. **Social Media:** Get all your friends involved. Create a Facebook page. Create a Twitter account. Get politicians to contribute information on the topic.

12. **Vote!** It is a great power rarely used by young people in civilizations where most needs are met. That is the best time to exercise your democratic right. Use your passion mission to change the world.

13. **See what happens:** Even if you do the first four on the list, you are making a difference. Anything after that and you are changing the world.

Find your passion mission!

Find it, research it, learn to discuss it, get others involved, and make it happen.

Start now! Write down three ideas that could change the world for the better, even if it's the smallest thing and no one else will notice. Choose one and put it on the mirror so it is the first thing you see in the morning. When you see it, say to yourself: I can make a difference and today I will do one thing that brings me closer to my goal.

How does that fill up that emptiness? When we start thinking about helping others, we raise not only their hopes but our own heart's desires. Our hearts rise up beyond the petty slights and missteps of daily life and begin to focus on a bigger picture—the image of belonging to a greater community. Is that love? Is that grace? I don't know but whatever it is, when you pay it forward, it grows. Try it. If you do it and it doesn't work, you've lost nothing; but if it does work, you may find something indescribable.

My passion mission is helping young adults rise above whatever keeps them stuck so that they may find their personal power. I work with clients, teach parents how to mentor, and talk to organizations on how to do the same for their employees.

It is what I do but it is also what I love doing. I enjoy seeing someone grow and become his or her best beyond what I could ever imagine.

Throughout this book, I have shared with you how small actions done on a daily basis can achieve great changes. I invite you now to bring that skill to helping others and watch your life transform to the best of what you can be.

Write me at *sgts@reallifecoaching.ca* and tell me what your passion misson is.

Epilogue

So you went from being a slacker with unrealized potential to a mover and shaker in 13 Steps. Or more likely, you just read this whole book (without skipping over too much, I hope) and you now have a bunch of questions. I will answer the reader's questions first and then get to the frequently asked questions for those who have experienced this process.

Reader's Questions:

    a.   How long does this take?

    b.   Does it really work?

    c.   What makes you qualified to tell me what to do?

    d.   How does one go about it?

    e.   How do you know it's working?

    f.   How do you know when you've arrived?

    g.   What are the best-case and worst-case scenarios?

These are really good questions and they are questions I do hear occasionally during the earlier stages of the process and quite often when we are close to a breakthrough.

a. **How long does it take?**

The first two Stages, Personal and Professional Development, can take as little as six months or as long as two years to complete. It really depends on how much resistance and negative mind-speak the client has to shovel away to become open to finding his or hers daily personal powers. Very often, once the client is on the right track, there will be one or two major diversions that will throw everything off. These distractions are to be expected as they are the inner-self testing to see if this thing that seems to be working is worth it. Stage Three, Inner Development, is a life-long pursuit.

b. **Does it really work?**

Short answer. Yes! It really does work. What makes it work is that in adhering to small, daily routines, we find our character and our faith in ourselves. We learn to transpose those character-building qualities into other aspects of our lives and figure out the modifications that need to be done. We learn that with a positive mental attitude and the will to work at it and learn from our mistakes, we can do anything. This is a sure-fire recipe for success because it comes from within.

c. **What makes you qualified to tell me what to do?**

Nothing. No one can tell you what to do. But having worked with struggling teens and young adults since 2001 and having seen their amazing successes, I do feel qualified to share my system with you. It is entirely your choice to decide to follow the system. You are in charge at all times and that is the best way.

d. **How does one go about it?**

I would read the whole book first. Then go through one chapter at a time, making notes and doing what the chapter suggests to you. The most important part will be getting a mentor and making sure that they are on the same page as you (literally). Most importantly, understand that mistakes and mess-ups contain the seeds to grow your greatest work. Don't give up and don't lose hope. I would also suggest keeping this process to yourself and a very select group of confidants. There are many people out there who live through their fears and can send out negative thoughts and ideas on any project. Let the people outside of your select group of confidants learn about it through the concrete results of your new successes. The others will discover the powerful "new you" through the transformations in your attitude, actions, and the successes in your life.

e. How do you know it's working?

In the first six months you are looking for micro-successes; you are not looking for the final "out in the world" results. For example, if you were often failing tests before and you have stopped failing tests but are just scraping by, note this as an improvement. It's not the end result you want, but it tells you that you are choosing not to fail. That is a big first step. You must first choose to embrace success (not fail). After that, you try stuff, mess up, all the while learning from the "mess-ups," but committing to do better next time. And then you raise your investment (the amount of time you work on what it is your are trying to improve) and see how that works. Adjust and refine. You know it's working because the micro-successes are there; you know it's working because you don't give up or retreat if you fail, but come back and repeat or modify.

f. How do you know when you've arrived?

For Steps one to 11 there are clear indications that you are ready to go on to the next step. When you can look over the chapter and know that you are succeeding in all the suggestions given to you, you are ready to move forward. As for your goals in following your bliss, creating a full life, and finding your passion mission, these are on-going, life-long projects. If you meet your target, you will want to create a new one. They represent your most meaningful endeavours on the journey of life.

g. What are the best-case and worst case scenarios?

The best-case scenario is you moving slowly and steadily through the process, building up a faith in your own ability to succeed under your own horsepower that will be with you for the rest of your life.

The worst-case scenario is when you start the process and finding it difficult or meeting a setback, you give up. Even in this scenario there is hope. You can always come back. You can always start again. You can always choose to give it one more try.

For those who have completed the 13 Steps

Congratulations! But, you don't really need any outside praise at this point because you believe in yourself now and, although it is nice to hear how well you are doing, you are no longer dependent on the good or bad comments of others. Your own inner-compass is the one you follow; the outside world becomes more of a radar blip to help you understand how your work is being regarded by others, and you will find that it reflects more about them than it does about you.

The big question for those who have completed the 13 Steps

This reminds me of my first dog Katie. She always wanted to catch a squirrel but was unable to do so in her first few attempts. After a while she realized that squirrels often hide on the other side of the tree trunk, so one day she just ran around to the other side, caught the squirrel off-guard and was able to grab him in her mouth. You could see in her eyes she was thinking... "Now that I've got him... what do I do?" (What's the next step?) Then there was a flash in her eyes where she figured out the next mouth watering step, at which point I yelled out "drop it." Katie let go, the squirrel bolted up the tree with a great story to tell his squirrelly friends.

Now that I have completed the book, what's the next step?

(First, let go of the squirrel!)

The next step is to bring your success skills into the following arenas: relationships, budgeting and investing, sales skills, nutrition and body-care, parenting, and business.

I will have books on these subjects in the coming while but I am always open to responding to any mail on any subject regarding your path towards success.

My weekly newsletter is a way to get my most recent articles on which-ever book I am working on and there is always place for feedback. You can get the newsletter by e-mailing newsletter@reallifecoaching.ca

The Mentors' Workbook

The Mentor's Workbook is the companion book to this method, and gives your mentor a deeper explanation on how to implement each step. The Workbook gives a lot of examples and it is as close as you can come to having me personally guide you through the process without your coming to one of my workshops or being one of my clients. The Workbook really opens up each Step.

In conclusion

I hope it's clear by this point how much I believe in this generation and the possibilities that exist for them in making a wonderful world worth living in. This is my passion mission and it is my hope that each and every one of you find your successes in life and have at the very least, one moment of bliss each and every day. May your journey be challenging, may your thoughts be of greatness, may you rise above your obstacles, and may you find your greatness, going farther than I could dare dream.

Thank you for sharing this time with me. Until we meet again… my best wishes to you for a happy and successful life…. And remember…

"A life worth living is a life lived willing to take risks"

~ Ken Rabow ~

Ken Rabow

17757730R00054

Made in the USA
Charleston, SC
27 February 2013